I Ran with the King

Kevin Ashley Pace
& Lauren Olivia Hennessey

TRILOGY
A WHOLLY OWNED SUBSIDIARY OF **TBN**
PROFESSIONAL PUBLISHING MEETS POWERFUL PROMOTION

Trilogy Christian Publishers
A Wholly Owned Subsidiary of Trinity Broadcasting Network
2442 Michelle Drive
Tustin, CA 92780

Copyright © 2025 Kevin Ashley Pace & Lauren Olivia Hennessey
Cover Art by Melissa LeeAnn Pace
All scripture quotations, unless otherwise noted, are taken from the ESV® Bible (The Holy Bible, English Standard Version®), copyright © 2001 by Crossway Bibles, a publishing ministry of Good News Publishers. Used with permission. All rights reserved.
All rights reserved, including the right to reproduce this book or portions thereof in any form whatsoever.
For information, address Trilogy Christian Publishing
Rights Department, 2442 Michelle Drive, Tustin, CA 92780.
Trilogy Christian Publishing/ TBN and colophon are trademarks of Trinity Broadcasting Network.
For information about special discounts for bulk purchases, please contact Trilogy Christian Publishing.
Trilogy Disclaimer: The views and content expressed in this book are those of the author and may not necessarily reflect the views and doctrine of Trilogy Christian Publishing or the Trinity Broadcasting Network.
10 9 8 7 6 5 4 3 2 1
Library of Congress Cataloging-in-Publication Data is available.
ISBN 979-8-89597-074-4
ISBN 979-8-89597-075-1 (ebook)

Dedication

To my girls.

To Melanie for her unending support.

To Lauren for her work to make this story readable.

To Melissa for her artistic talents.

Preface

This is a short work of fiction, written by a man with little experience with literature. Yet, for this story, literary experience seemed less important than biblical inspiration. While most of the story came from my own imagination, I tried to present the character of God as accurately as possible. It is my desire that this simple read draws you into a deeper relationship with our loving Lord and Savior. I want to express my personal gratitude to my wife and daughters, who continue to inspire me to live a life worthy of our calling. I love each of you so very much.

Table of Contents

Prologue 11

Chapter One: The Son. 13

Chapter Two: The Murder. 21

Chapter Three: The Carpenter. 25

Chapter Four: The Child 35

Chapter Five: The Scholar 49

Chapter Six: The Friend 55

Chapter Seven: The Miracle Man. 61

Chapter Eight: The Good Shepherd 67

Chapter Nine: The Betrayal 73

Chapter Ten: The Crucifixion 85

Chapter Eleven: One More Race 91

Prologue

Winter. The coldest and darkest time of the year. For years, it reached out with its cold arms and dragged me into a season of despair. My hatred — towards myself for not being a better father and protector, towards the king for his cruelty, towards El Shaddai for allowing it to happen — has finally diminished. But I have yet to shake away my anger and grief. Years later, and I am still haunted by the memory of that night. When I sleep, I relive the horrors in my dreams. I close my eyes, and flashes of fiery red light dance behind my eyes. I can hear the screams of terror intermingled with cheers. I remember the shock I felt. How could our king do this to his people? I remember the betrayal. How could Yahweh, our God of peace and love, allow this to happen?

CHAPTER ONE:

The Son

When I was a very young man, I was a shepherd. My father taught me how to take care of the sheep, and I always felt at peace in the fields. The sheep have such a complete trust in the shepherd, turning to him when they are sick, injured, or even frightened. I loved spending time alone in the wilderness with the animals. Especially after my father died when I was just a teenager. It gave me time to grieve privately.

I was still a shepherd when I met Mira. Her father had recently acquired land from his neighbor and a small herd of sheep along with it. He hired me to add his sheep to my much larger flock. When I came to collect his sheep, Mira was washing clothes in their front yard. She was beautiful. Her dark hair blew behind her in the wind, and her arms looked slender but strong. I approached her and caught sight of her bright, smiling eyes before she dropped her gaze. She welcomed me to her home and asked if she could get me anything to eat or drink before I returned to the fields with my flock. Her voice was soft and sweet, like a song. I shared a small loaf of bread with her and a cup of water before leaving. I was struck by her kindness and her hospitality.

I saw her regularly for several months, as I continued to bring her father's sheep back to him. Eventually, I spoke to her father about my intentions with her, and we became engaged. We loved each other, and we knew how blessed we both were to have met. We were soon married, and she moved into my family's house, where I lived with my mother. Our first few years of marriage were such happy ones. El Roi blessed us. We lived on beautiful land, where the flock would graze. I would come in from the fields, and Mira would be waiting for me with a warm and delicious meal prepared. She and I would talk every night before bed while she was weaving or sewing. As our marriage matured, Mira began to talk about having a baby. We both wanted a child badly.

We prayed for five years, offering sacrifices and begging Yahweh-Yireh for His blessing. It was especially hard on Mira. Every month, she grew more discouraged. She would cling to me and cry, convinced Yahweh was punishing her for her sins or her lack of faith. I would remind her of the stories of Sarah, mother of Isaac, and Rachel, mother of Joseph and Benjamin, and Hannah, mother of Samson. But I too was losing hope. Then our prayers were finally answered. Yahweh-Yireh blessed us with a beautiful son. Our joy was indescribable.

For months, we prepared for the arrival of our long-awaited baby. Mira wove a beautiful quilt of bright colors, and I fashioned a cradle out of cypress. It was one of my earliest carpentry projects and was definitely not a thing of beauty. But Mira was so proud. She relished talking to her friends about the joys and hardships of being with child. We would lie in bed together, looking at the corner of our room where we had set up everything for our coming child and discussing names and imagining our future together.

Our son was born in the early summer. We named him Joshua after my father. My mother wept when she found out. She helped deliver him and was the first to hold him. She beamed at him and raised her eyes to heaven, giving thanks and praising Jehovah. Joshua was her only grandson, and she was convinced he was perfect.

When my mother died, Joshua was four months old. On the morning she died, I cradled Joshua and remembered how she had held him. She held him as if she held the future. I looked into his eyes, so much like his mother's, and he smiled back at me. It was the first time he smiled at me like he meant it. Like he recognized me as his father, and he loved me. I remember praying that night after I tucked him into his crib, wrapping him gently. I thanked Yahweh for giving us this child. For trusting us to raise him in the Lord's ways. I dedicated him again, in my mind, to the work of God.

Joshua almost didn't have a peaceful entrance into the world. A few weeks before his birth, we traveled to Bethlehem for the census. The crowds were overwhelming, and we had not planned accordingly. Mira was eight months pregnant and extremely uncomfortable. Anxious to provide some sort of relief, I left her behind and ran ahead. Inn after inn, every place was full. Tempers were running high, and I began to grow afraid for my pregnant wife. I prayed, pleading with God that she might not go into labor while we were in this unfamiliar city and that we wouldn't have to sleep on the streets. Finally, I found an innkeeper who agreed to give us his last available room. I ran quickly back through the streets and brought Mira back with me. The innkeeper's wife escorted her to our room while I took our donkey out to the barn. Before I got inside, I could hear voices coming from the other side of the door.

I opened the door tentatively and immediately lowered my eyes in shame. "I'm so sorry. I didn't realize anyone was in here." A man stood over his young wife who was in active labor. He bent down and whispered something in her ear before coming over to meet me in the doorway.

He smiled. His eyes were kind. "It's alright. I'm sure you weren't expecting anything like this in a stable." I nodded, keeping my eyes downcast. "The innkeeper ran out of rooms but was kind enough to offer us his barn because my wife's time has come. I'll lead your donkey to a stall. Would you mind finding the innkeeper's wife for us? We would appreciate some blankets and boiled water."

"Yes, of course," I stammered. His wife let out a cry of pain, and he turned hastily away from me and returned to her side.

I cannot imagine how he could be so calm in this situation. If it were my Mira lying in the hay like that, I would be in a panic. I went quickly to find the innkeeper's wife and then returned to our room to tell Mira what I had seen.

"Oh, Hatach!" she cried. "Those poor people! Imagine if it were us in that stable." She stood suddenly, quite a feat while balancing her large belly, and reached into a satchel. She pulled out the quilt she had been weaving for our child. She had finally completed it.

"Here, I want you to take this to them," she said. I raised my eyebrows in surprise. I knew how much time she had spent on this quilt. She chose the colors carefully and had been imagining it softening my crudely carved cradle. But she insisted. She said this family needed something soft to swaddle their soon-coming baby in.

I carried the blanket back out to the barn and knocked on the door. The man opened it just a crack and looked surprised to see me again.

"This is for you," I said, extending the quilt out to him. "I know it is not much, but my wife wanted you to have it for your baby."

"Thank you, and shalom," he said gratefully. He took the blanket, and we bowed quickly to each other before he turned away again and went to his wife's side. I breathed a silent prayer for that couple and for their baby as I walked back to our room in the inn. Looking back, I wish I had done more. I wish I had volunteered to give them our room. I'm ashamed of my own selfishness.

Luckily, my Mira did not give birth while we were in Bethlehem. We made it back to our home in Jezreel, and Joshua was born two short weeks later. My mother placed him on Mira's chest and then allowed us privacy to meet our son. I lay next to her. We counted his fingers and toes and marveled at his beauty.

"He looks like you," Mira whispered, her voice thick with emotion. I wiped a tear from my own eyes.

When I held him for the first time, I couldn't control my emotions. I praised God, blessed my wife, and spoke gently to my son. I thought again of the baby born in a barn and hoped he was as healthy as Joshua.

Life, at that moment, was perfect. And the next year was full of the happiest days I've ever known. Every day was another day of watching Joshua learn and grow. He was an incredibly happy baby, hardly crying, and content to be swaddled onto his Ima's back as she went through her day. Most mornings, I would take him from his cradle and take him outside before Mira woke up. I would give him warm milk and watch the sun rise with him on my lap. I talked to him constantly. I told him about the sheep and which ones were looking best for the season. I told him how they needed to be fed and taken care of. I talked to him about the proper breeding techniques. He should never combine two particular breeds, and he should only keep a certain number of male sheep in the herd. I told him all about the trees. Which made the best building materials, where they could be found, and how they were identified. He would coo at me, and I am certain he knew me. His father. I knew he was going to be a greater man than me.

Sometimes, the thought of being responsible for such a small and helpless life overwhelmed me. One particular morning that feeling felt so powerful. I raised Joshua above my head and prayed. Prayed that Adoni would protect him. Prayed for wisdom and guidance. Prayed that my son would lead a life that was pleasing and glorifying to God.

In the following years, I thought back on that prayer and felt a stab in my chest. I felt like Yahweh had betrayed me and failed my son.

CHAPTER TWO:

The Murder

I jolted awake. Mira was already sitting up. Even in the darkness, I could sense the fear radiating from her.

"Something is wrong, Hatach," she said.

I heard a loud banging on the door downstairs and realized that must have been what woke us up. Suddenly, there was a louder crashing noise, and I could hear footsteps pounding through our kitchen. Mira shrieked, and I leapt out of bed.

I made it to the door of our room and saw soldiers climbing up the ladder towards us.

The burly man leading the charge bared his teeth at me and brandished his sword. I stumbled back in shock and confusion and turned back to face Mira. She was sitting on the bed, eyes closed, lips moving in silent prayer. She held Joshua clutched to her chest, and he was crying. I remember thinking that wasn't good. He needed to be quiet so the soldiers might not find him. Of course, that wouldn't have made a difference.

The men made it to the top of the ladder. I threw my arms out as if to block the view of my exposed wife and vulnerable son.

"Please," I begged. "What do you want? Take anything, anything. We've always been obedient to the throne. We've always— " My pleas were cut off as I was kicked hard in the knees and then shoved to the ground. From there, I couldn't see what was happening. I could only hear the cries of my wife and child.

The soldiers ordered Mira to hand Joshua to them. When she refused, they used a club to beat her over the head. Even when she fell back, she kept her arms wrapped around our son. The men violently wrenched Joshua from her arms. And using a sword, they murdered him. Right in front of her. Her scream was unlike anything I've ever heard. It was a sound of total agony and despair. That is the sound I hear in my nightmares.

The soldiers tossed my son to the ground and rushed out of the room to go on to the next house. I crawled to Joshua and held him close. Mira joined us on the floor. I began to sing a lullaby to him, trying to keep my voice steady. Mira used her hands to gently trace a circle across his cheek and up and down his arms. Joshua grew quiet and still, then breathed his last shuddering breath in my arms. I broke down. I sobbed, unable to catch my breath. Certain that I would never be able to breathe normally again.

Mira clung to me and cried, hardly noticing the blood running from her forehead down her face. As the night went on, more screams filled the air until it was like one voice, weeping and letting out pained lamentation, as mothers became childless.[1]

Mira didn't stop crying until Joshua was buried two days later. We buried him in the fields, surrounded by sheep. Mira turned numb. She stopped crying. She stopped eating. She stopped responding to me. She stopped getting up in the morning. I would scoop her into my arms and carry her around. No matter how I begged or cried, she did not seem to notice that I was there. Nothing made her smile. The only time she showed any sign of emotion was in her sleep: she would wake up screaming in the night. I knew that she was picturing the soldiers slashing into our son, hearing his last rasping breath. I have the same dreams.

She died three agonizing weeks later, whether from her head injury or just losing the will to live, I was never sure. I was left to mourn the loss of my son and the loss of my wife. I moved days after burying her because staying

---
1 Matthew 2:18, ESV

in that house was taking too much of an emotional toll on me. I couldn't stand to be in the same kitchen where she once cooked or sleep in the same room without her. I couldn't look at Joshua's crib without envisioning his cold and lifeless body in it.

The only thing I knew to do was to submerge myself in work and stay busy. I wanted complete separation from the happy life I had once known. I sold all my sheep, moved to Nazareth, and became a businessman. I used my profits from selling my flock to buy lumber, and I began supplying lumber for multiple building projects in our town. It was this new job that led me to the most incredible friendship. One that helped me more than anything in overcoming my bitterness and grief.

CHAPTER THREE:

The Carpenter

I heard footsteps and knew someone had entered my shop. I put down my saw and began clapping the sawdust off my hands when I heard a voice behind me.

"Shalom. You must be Hatach," the man's voice rang out. I turned and studied him. He was a Hebrew man with sharp features and a full beard. He was around my height but stood taller, as though he bore no burdens. I could not quite place his face.

"Shalom," I bowed slightly, racking my brain to figure out who this man could be. "Yes, that's me. Is all well with you?"

"Yes, thank you. My name is Joseph. I'm here to inquire about some business," he continued.

"Wonderful!" I exclaimed. "Right this way. Let me pour you some fresh halitot, and we can discuss business in my home." My house was divided into two sections. The front half functioned as my wood shop, and the back half was the space that I lived in. I led him out of the shop and into my house.

I gestured for him to lounge at my table and busied myself in the kitchen. I had a fire going, so it only took a few minutes to bring water to a boil for the halitot. I poured us each a cup and sat at the table with him.

"Thank you," he said after taking a sip.

"What can I help you with?" I asked.

"Well," he crossed his arms on the table. "I am a carpenter. I actually used to live in this town, and I oversaw most of the building projects here."

I opened my mouth, confused. I had been working here in Nazareth for around three years at the time, and I was well acquainted with all the carpenters here. I knew I had never seen this man in any of the shops that I supplied lumber for. That was not where I recognized him from.

"No worries, my friend," he said, sensing my confusion. "I have been living in Egypt for three years. From what I have heard, you arrived in Nazareth just a few weeks after I left."

I nodded, "Yes, I have been here for quite some time now." I wasn't sure if he was looking for more explanation, but I didn't want to discuss the reason for my move. I took another sip of my halitot.

"My wife and I have returned to Nazareth, and we intend to stay here for many years and raise our family here. I would love to partner with you to build our home."

It was when he mentioned his wife that I suddenly realized who this was. I had a flashback to a man standing at the entrance to a stable and his wife lying on the hay behind him. This was the man from that night in Bethlehem. I shook my head slightly to clear my head, knowing that I couldn't dwell on that memory without spiraling into ones that were much more painful. He noticed my head shaking and thought I was disinterested in his business.

"Oh, I'm sorry!" I apologized, embarrassed by my daydreaming. "My thoughts were somewhere else. But I would love to help you with your home. Let's talk about the plans for it. What are you envisioning, as far as building materials and size?" Joseph and I sat for a long time together, discussing the plans for his house. In my head, I felt that if I could make his home well, I could make up for not offering my room at the inn to him and his wife.

Joseph rose from the table, "Thank you, Hatach," he bowed. "I look forward to doing business with you. I must leave now to make it in time for the evening meal with my family."

I rose to bow in response and wish him well but then he spoke again.

"Actually, would you like to join us? We would be delighted if you and your wife shared a meal with us tonight."

"No, thank you for the invite, but—"

"I'm being sincere. We would love it so much if you would join us," Joseph said. I was going to refuse again, but I had been lonely for three years. I craved this man's friendship. So, I found myself agreeing.

"As long as it's no trouble for you," I began.

Joseph cut me off, "Of course, it's no trouble. Mary always makes plenty of food, and it's good, too. There will be plenty for you and your wife."

"It's just me, actually," I said. Joseph looked puzzled for a moment. "It's just me. My wife passed away a few years ago, just before I moved to Nazareth." "Oh, Hatach. I'm so sorry. I had no idea. I—"

"But I'd still love to go and share the evening meal with you," I said.

He relaxed and smiled. "I'm so glad. Walk with me, Hatach. It isn't far."

"Tell me about your family, Joseph," I asked him as we began to walk up the road. His eyes lit up.

"I met Mary about five years ago. I was instantly struck by her kind and calm spirit. She had a kind of peace about her. At the time, I was still an apprentice. But I asked for her hand, and we remained betrothed until I had earned enough denarii to support her. We've been through a couple of tough times together, but I am so grateful that El Shaddai blessed me with her as my wife. I cannot imagine walking through those difficulties with anybody else." He ended with his gaze turned upward, as though he might be thanking God right there. I was uncomfortable. It had been many years since I had prayed.

"And we have a son," Joseph added, pride edging his words. "He is three years old and the most precious child you can imagine. His name is Jesus."

I felt a lump growing in my throat. His child had survived. The child born in that dirty stable survived and somehow escaped Herod's brutal decree. How could one be evil enough to order the execution of male children? It was unfathomable. I wanted to stop Joseph right there and ask him how he did it. How had he protected his wife and child during that horrible time?

But there was no time for questions like that. We arrived at the house Joseph and his family were temporarily staying in, and Joseph welcomed me inside.

I was struck immediately, as we stepped in, with the scent of food being prepared. Mary was over at the fire, but when she saw us walk in, she came over to greet us.

"Shalom," she said, bowing to me. I bowed back.

"Mary, this is Hatach, the lumber supplier I told you about. He agreed to help me build our home. I invited him to join us for the evening meal tonight."

Mary lifted her eyes to look at mine. I understood then what Joseph had said about her earlier. Her countenance seemed almost serene, as though she understood that everything happening around her was planned.

"Hatach," she said warmly. "How wonderful to have you join us tonight. Please, sit down. The meal is almost prepared."

"Thank you, Mary," I said. Joseph pointed out the cushion intended for me, and I sat. Suddenly, in toddled a boy, dragging a small blanket behind him. When he saw his father, he dropped the blanket and ran up to him. I squinted at the blanket. It was a bit tattered and faded, but I would have recognized it anywhere. That was the blanket Mira had made. The one I gave to Joseph through the stable door on the night his son was born. I couldn't believe they still had it. I had to restrain myself from going to pick it up and holding it to my face. I wanted to breathe it in and smell the lingering scent of Mira's perfume and rub my cheek along it to feel the stitches she made.

Meanwhile, Joseph bent and scooped Jesus up in his arms and tossed him into the air. Jesus giggled uncontrollably, and Mary smiled as she watched them. I smiled too, but mine was more bittersweet.

"Jesus, come meet our new friend, Hatach," Joseph said as he put him down. He walked hand-in-hand with Jesus over to where I was lounging at the table.

"Shalom," Jesus said. I smiled at his manners. Mary brought the bread and wine and fish to the table.

"Come on, Jesus; it's time to eat," Joseph said. "Can I sit next to you?" Jesus asked me.

"Of course," I patted the cushion next to myself. Jesus sat down dutifully, and Mary and Joseph took their places at the table. I was waiting for one of them to pass me a dish when I noticed their bowed heads. I quickly bowed mine, not wanting them to notice I had forgotten the custom of praying before a meal.

"Yahweh," Joseph began, "We come to you this day with hearts very full. Thank you for your blessings in our lives. Thank you for Hatach, and may you be with him. We thank you for this food, and we pray that you will guide us to your will. Amen."

"Amen," Mary echoed. Then, they began to pass the dishes around.

They asked me many questions, which I usually dodged to avoid talking to people about Mira and Joshua. But there was something different about them that made me want to open up to them. I wanted them to know me. I told them that my family was from Bethlehem, like theirs. That I was just a lumber supplier, not a carpenter, because I had never figured out how to take a lump of wood and turn it into anything worth selling. I told them how I shepherded in Jezreel when I was a younger man and that it was this which brought me to Mira. I told them that I named my son after my father, and that Joshua would have been just the same age as their Jesus. I shared briefly that I had lost my Joshua and Mira within weeks of each other.

Mary and Joseph listened attentively. They both seemed to have this deep understanding about them. They were truly compassionate.

At the end of the meal, I thanked Mary for her hospitality and told her how much I enjoyed the food. Then I rose to say farewell. Jesus stood right in front of me.

"Shalom," I said and bowed just my head. "Thank you for letting me join you and your family tonight, Jesus."

Jesus shrugged. "You should come all the time," he said. I laughed. Joseph walked me out their door.

"Jesus is right, you know," he said when we got outside. "You should come all the time. It's been a pleasure getting to know you, and I am so glad we will be doing business together."

"Yes, I am too," I said, smiling.

"I will remember you in my prayers," Joseph said. "Shalom."

"Shalom," I bowed. I could not bring myself to say I would pray for this family. Although they reminded me tonight of what I once believed about Yahweh, they also reminded me what had been taken from me. I know Mira and Mary would have gotten along. Mira would have enjoyed having a friend to swap recipes with and weave baskets and blankets with. I was several years older than Joseph, but Mary seemed to be several years younger than my Mira. I knew Mira would have seen her like a little sister. She would have brought Joshua with her to Mary's house, so he and Jesus could play together. She would have relished every opportunity to tell someone about his newest words and fascinations. I could've helped Joseph build his house, with a room just for Jesus and his future brothers and sisters. And then Joseph would've done the same for me.

That night, I tossed for hours before finally falling asleep. And while I slept, I dreamed of Joshua. In my dream, he was much older. He was running through a field, smiling, and laughing. I watched him run, and then called his name. He stopped when he heard and turned my way.

"Run to me, Joshua!" I called; my arms open wide.

"Abba, I can't run to you," he said. "But I have incredible news for you: the King is alive! Run with Him!"

I woke up, and my cheeks were wet with tears. It was like the vision of my son's face had been stamped on the back of my eyelids. And I couldn't stop hearing those words coming from his mouth. I had no idea what my son was speaking of, but I remembered the dream for years after.

CHAPTER FOUR:

The Child

Over the next several years, I grew closer and closer to Joseph and his family. We finished his house just in time for Jesus' little brother, James, to be welcomed into the family. I held little James a few days after he was born and was reminded of holding my own son. I began to weep, holding baby James close to my chest. Joseph did not say anything but simply put his hand on my shoulder and allowed me to cry.

I eventually regained control over my emotions. Embarrassed, I passed the baby back to Mary and was prepared to leave.

"Just a minute, I'll walk with you," Joseph said.

"I'm sorry," I said when we got outside. "I didn't realize that would affect me so much. It's just that... I haven't held a baby since the night Joshua died." I looked up as we walked, trying to prevent any tears from spilling out.

"Oh, friend," Joseph said, again placing a hand on my shoulder. "I apologize. I was just so proud to show our baby off, I didn't even consider what it would make you feel."

"No," I swallowed. "It's not your fault. And I'm honored to be one of the first to hold him. He is a beautiful boy."

Joseph nodded, and we walked in silence for a few moments. Then, he said, "I wanted to tell you about the time my family spent in Egypt."

I looked over at him, feeling like this was a strange time to bring that up. But I agreed.

"Mary and I traveled to Bethlehem for the census many years ago —" here another pang of guilt hit me as I remembered again my failure to help him and his wife "— and Jesus was born while we were there. A few nights after he was born, I had the most vivid dream. It was a vision from El Olam. I was warned not to return home to Nazareth but to escape instead to Egypt. When Mary woke up that morning, I had our belongings prepared, and we began the journey immediately. We lived in Egypt until Herod's death. Then, we decided it was safe to return home."[2]

I remembered Herod's death. I would be lying if I

---

2 Matthew 2:13-15, ESV

didn't confess to the surge of satisfaction I felt when I first heard the news. And many of the others living in my town felt the same way. The Romans, to honor their fallen hero, had a parade, and I thought I would be sick as I saw his body pass my house.

He continued, "But this wasn't the first vision I received from Yahweh. I had one a few years before that, too. Before Jesus was born. Jesus is not actually my child. Mary became pregnant with him before we were married." I looked at him in shock. He wasn't Jesus' real father. I gawked, silently wondering if I would have married Mira if she was going to have another man's baby. He continued, "When I found out, I was devastated, and I felt like I couldn't marry her. I was planning to put her away quietly with no shame[3] when I received a dream from El Olam. An angel spoke to me and told me that Jesus is the Son of God, conceived by His Spirit. He told me to name him Jesus because He will be the savior of the world.[4] I don't pretend to understand exactly what that means or what my son's purpose is here. But I believe he was placed in my life and in this world for great things according to God's plan. I know Yahweh is faithful. I know He will be steadfast, and He will continue to guide my family."

We reached my house. I was confused and startled. Was Joseph claiming that Jesus was the Messiah? I knew

---

3 Matthew 1:19, ESV
4 Matthew 1:20-23, ESV

him to be a very devout man who would not be guilty of blasphemy. Yet it seemed like this is what he was implying.

"I know this is difficult to understand, and I don't expect you to have a response," Joseph said. "But as one of my closest friends, I wanted you to know. I hope you can come to understand this great truth with me. I will see you again soon, Hatach. Shalom."

I would ponder his words in my mind often as we grew closer. I was accepted as a part of this family very quickly. Mary always extended a warm dinner invitation to me. I wasn't much of a cook, but I would sometimes bring their family a loaf of bread or a fresh wineskin. And as Jesus grew older, he would sometimes stop by my shop. Even as a young boy, he was learning the trade from his father, so he would come to show me something new that he had learned. He had a certain style of carpentry. While most people would hide the scarred wood on the underside of their works, Jesus put the scars on display. He told me he thought the scars gave the product a special beauty. And he was right. His style was easily recognizable, and all of his works were unique.

He started calling me Papa Hatach.

As I grew closer to them, I found myself opening my heart again. Slowly. I would join them at the temple on the Sabbath. I began praying again. I started to tithe. I started to trust in Jehovah-Jireh as I had many years ago.

One day, after I finished my morning meal, I heard the shouts of children playing in the streets. I looked out my window. They were reenacting a scene from a great battle. I stood watching them for a moment, then spotted Jesus, who was around twelve years old at this time. Concentration was etched on his face as he began to sling his hand above his head as though he were holding a slingshot. He let it go, and the boy opposite him, standing high above the others on the street railing, fell off and stumbled back, obviously struck by the invisible stone. All the other children ran around, celebrating the victory and cheering. Except for Jesus. The victor, who should be the loudest of them all. He tilted his head back and spoke to the heavens. I furrowed my brow at his response.

When he returned his gaze to its normal height, he spotted me in the window. He waved for me to come out and join them.

"Papa Hatach!" he cried. "Will you please teach my friends the game you taught me a few weeks ago?"

I smiled and hurried outside, stopping to grab a piece of lifeless coal from my oven. I walked out and met the small crowd of boys.

"Shalom, boys," I greeted them. I got a disjointed chorus back at me. "So, you all want to learn to play square ball?"

"Yes, please," they responded. Then, I began drawing a square on the cobblestone. I explained the rules and how they should stand and toss the ball to each other.

I straightened back up. Jesus smiled at me. "Thank you, Papa Hatach."

"Of course. You boys have a fun time out here," I turned to go back into my house.

"Do you want to play a round with us?" Jesus asked. I wavered for a moment. I had work I needed to start on. But if my Joshua were alive, he would be playing with those boys. With that realization, I agreed.

I got into the square with the other boys and waited for the first pass. As we played, I was continuously struck by Jesus' attitude. When the other boys tagged somebody "out," they would gloat and sometimes tease the one who was tagged for being too slow. Jesus was just as good as the other boys, but when he made a good move, he never acted prideful or called the loser names. And he didn't act superior or bored; he was full of laughter and smiles, clearly enjoying the game. He was fun to play with. I played five rounds of square ball with the boys, and I loved every minute of it. But I knew I had to get back to work. When I got out on the last round, I wished them well and went back into my house. Even from my carpentry shop, I could still hear their shouts of joy from the road.

Hours later, I heard a knock on my shop door. Jesus walked in, flushed from playing outside.

"Shalom, Jesus," I greeted him.

"Shalom, Papa Hatach."

"Do you have a new carpentry skill to show me?" I asked.

"No, not today. I have an invitation to extend to you. My Ima and Abba would like to invite you to travel with our family to Jerusalem for the Festival of the Passover this year. We will start the journey in two weeks' time."

"Well... I don't know. I've just started making a new product. I'm getting a lot of business with it, and I'm not sure if I need to take three weeks off to go to Jerusalem this year," I said.

"What new product?" Jesus asked. "I've started supplying the execution crosses for the Roman government. One of the Roman centurions came in the other day and told me I had been selected to oversee their production," I said.

Jesus was quiet for a moment. I couldn't blame him if he were taken aback. If it had truly been my decision, I would not have wanted to make these crosses. But I know better than many that you cannot defy the orders of the king.

"Have you ever been to the prison?" Jesus asked.

"No, of course not," I said.

"Well, I have," Jesus said. I looked at him, startled. What was this twelve-year-old doing in the prisons? "I go sometimes and talk to the people before they're executed. They are hopeless and desperate, in need of compassion. Most of the time, even their family has abandoned them. I go and listen to their stories and tell them about the hope found in Yahweh. Lots of times, they sit in the back of their cell and don't listen. But sometimes, they'll come up close to the bar. And they listen as though they know their lives depend on it. You should go sometime. Meet some of the people who end up on your crosses."

Before I had time to respond, he looked back up at me with a twinkle in his eyes. "And you should definitely go to Jerusalem with us." I laughed. "I'll think about it. Let me consider it and talk to your father about it."

Jesus agreed and then left. When he was gone, I considered what he had said. In fact, for several days, I couldn't get it out of my head. Finally, mid-chopping one day, I tossed my tools down onto the table and headed into the live-in portion of my home. I grabbed a loaf of fresh challah and headed out the door. I was going to the prison.

When I got there, I approached the guards standing at the door.

"What is your business here?" asked the first guard.

"I'm here to see a prisoner," I said.

"Name?"

"Hatach."

His eyes scanned his list. "There's no one here with that name."

"Oh, you mean the name of the prisoner I want to see. Actually, I-I..." I stammered, embarrassed. "I wanted to talk with someone who needed encouragement. Would that be okay?"

The guard snorted, "They all need encouragement here. That's fine if that's what you wish. Follow me." He opened the heavy door and led me down a narrow passage. Already, I was pursing my lips against the stench and the flies buzzing around.

Jesus was right. These people were hopeless. I expected them to shout at me when I entered their hall or approached the edge of their cells. But they hardly even looked up when I walked by. One man was weeping silently. Another was so emaciated I could see all his ribs and blood seeped out of cuts all along his back. The entire hall was eerily quiet. My footsteps slowed, and I was beginning to fear I had made a terrible mistake in coming here. I found myself wishing that Jesus had come with me. Though he was just a boy, I felt he would know better what to say in this case than I did.

After walking by several cells, the guard came to an abrupt stop. "Here you go. This is Titus. You may speak with him for a few minutes."

I waited for the guard to walk away before I cleared my throat. "Shalom," I called quietly through the bars. I heard a scoff in response. Undeterred, I continued on. "I brought e challah. It isn't warm, but I made it yesterday, so it's still fresh. I just thought you and I could enjoy it together today."

I broke off a braid of the challah and passed it through the bars. The inmate didn't move. I kept my hand outstretched with the bread in it for several moments. Eventually, I tossed it onto the thin cushion in the cell. I began to eat my own piece. I suddenly realized I didn't come with much of a plan about what I should say. I decided to start with an introduction.

"My name is Hatach. I'm a carpenter here. My young friend Jesus sent me." At this, he looked up in recognition. "You know Jesus?" I asked, eagerly.

"Yes," he said. I waited for him to say more, but he didn't. He looked back down at his feet.

"You met him here in prison?" I asked.

"Yes," he said again. This was not going well. How did Jesus, a child, do this? We sat in silence for a few more moments, and the prisoner picked up his bread and began to eat it.

"Want to know what I did?" he asked after several more minutes. My eyes widened in surprise. He continued, "I used to be a mercenary for our great king Herod, may he rest in peace. I was feared and adored. I served the king faithfully, protecting uprisings, killing children."

My mind reeled. What was I doing here? This man killed children! Did he kill my Joshua? My body turned to steel, and I felt a knot rising in my throat.

"Under the new king, my stock in this kingdom dropped significantly. I was no longer held in such favor. I didn't get the same special treatment. I struggled to support my wife and daughters and even fell into debt. I stole denarii from other mercenaries' pay to survive. But I was caught and thrown in here. Sentenced to death," he chuckled darkly. "Tomorrow is my execution day, actually.

"For almost a year, I sat here, dreading that day. Cursing the king for his selfishness. Dreaming of a way I could get out of here and take my revenge. I was full of hate, and anger, and bitterness, and fear," he said.

I whispered, "Was? How do you not still feel this way?"

He stood and approached the bars dividing us. "A few days ago, I had another visitor. Some call him Rabbi though he is still a boy. You know him as Jesus. He changed me, Hatach. He taught me about El Elyon and His love for His flock. He taught me about true forgiveness and mercy and showed me how to seek it for myself and the horrible sins I committed when I was under the king's command. That is how I can say truthfully that I am no longer full of bitterness towards the king. Jesus showed me to forgive as I am forgiven.[5] I pray for the king now, that he will come to know the truth as I do. Because of Jesus, I now know my future. Yes, I will be crucified tomorrow, but my story will not end. I am prepared for eternity."

I closed my eyes and thought of my Joshua. Where was he spending eternity? Would I see him there? I longed to ask Titus more about what Jesus had told him and about this peace he described, but the guard was coming back down the hall.

---

5 Eph. 4:32, ESV

"Thank you, Titus," I said before allowing myself to be led away. As I left, I glanced out of one of the windows and noticed a row of crosses lined up against the clay wall. My crosses.

I walked straight to Joseph's house. I waited impatiently at the door to be let in. Mary opened the door and said, "Hatach! I'm sorry, I wasn't expecting you today. Please, come in," she said.

"Shalom, Mary," I said quickly. "No, thank you. I just came to say that I would like to join your family when you all travel to Jerusalem for the Passover."

Mary broke out into a smile. She again had that peaceful look about her. I felt another pang as I wished my Mira could have met her.

"I am so happy to hear that, Hatach. And I know Joseph will be too. Are you sure you cannot stay for dinner tonight?"

"No, no. I really must be getting back. I really did not get much work done today. I just wanted to let you know as soon as I could. And let me know what I need to do for the preparations."

"Of course, Hatach. Shalom," she bowed.

As I walked home, my thoughts were racing. I hadn't been to Jerusalem for Passover since before Joshua was born. I made different excuses every year. An injured leg. Business demands. But it was really that I couldn't bear to go to the Temple. The Temple where Joshua was dedicated. Where it was expected that you pray and make sacrifices to Yahweh. But my heart had been softening these twelve years. And I felt ready to return. In fact, I felt guilty for not returning sooner. I breathed a quick prayer of rededication under my breath. A psalm I remembered from my younger days.

> *"Yes, my soul, find rest in God;*
> *My hope comes from him.*
> *Truly he is my rock and my salvation;*
> *He is my fortress, I will not be shaken.*
> *My salvation and my honor depend on God;*
> *He is my mighty rock, my refuge.*
> *Trust in him at all times, you people;*
> *Pour out your hearts to him,*
> *For God is our refuge."*[6]

---

6 Psalms 62:5-8, ESV

CHAPTER FIVE:

The Scholar

"Are we close yet?" asked Simon, one of Jesus' brothers. He was sitting on my shoulders as I walked.

I laughed and looked at the horizon. "You see that mound just at the edge of the horizon?"

Simon squinted and said, "I think so."

"That's it," I replied. "We will be there by tomorrow afternoon. And then the Festival begins!" A few hours later, Jesus fell into step with me.

"I'm so glad you decided to travel with us," he said.

"Me too," I responded. "I've been putting it off for far too many years. I've needed this for longer than I realized."

Jesus nodded, understanding in his young eyes. "I know this may be a difficult week for you. But I have been praying to my Abba for you. I know He will give you the peace and the strength you are searching for."

I was puzzled by Jesus' words. What did he mean, he had been praying to his father? And I had never even told him about losing my Joshua. Joseph must have told him, or perhaps he overheard us talking one day and remembered. Before I could ask anything, he ran up to join some children from a different family.

One day later, we reached the city. Joseph had arranged for us all to stay with a friend of his. We spent the next seven days eating together, visiting the Temple, making sacrifices, and reading the Scriptures. I spent the week in frequent prayer. And Jesus was right. Even when I went into the Temple and was hit with flashbacks from dedicating Joshua, I felt peaceful. I knew Yahweh was good. I knew He would provide for me as he did my ancestors long ago when they escaped Egypt.

After a happy week, the morning came for us to leave town. Everyone was rushing around, packing, and saying good-bye to friends. Joseph grabbed my arm as he and I passed each other in the hallway.

"Hatach, are you ready to leave?" he asked me.

"Yes, I have packed all my things. It's much quicker when you're just getting your own things and not your children's things, too," I said. I didn't want Joseph to think I was getting impatient with him.

"Mary and I want to walk down to an old friend's house this morning. If you're ready, you could leave now, and she and I will meet up with you at tonight's camp."

I considered for a moment. "Sure, that's fine. Would you like for me to take the kids with me?"

Joseph nodded gratefully, "If you don't mind keeping up with them, that would be a great help for Mary and me."

"I don't mind at all."

"Ok, we'll have them ready. I'll see you tonight at camp. Shalom. Travel safely."

"Shalom."

I headed out to the stable to saddle my donkey. When he was prepared, I went back into the house to get Joseph's children. James, Simon, and Jude were all waiting at the door.

"We're ready, Papa Hatach!" James cried.

"Let's go, then," I smiled, looking at their beaming faces. "Wait a minute. Where's Jesus?"

"Oh, he left earlier," Simon said.

I frowned. "Did he go with your parents?"

"I'm not sure," said Simon.

"Yes, he did," volunteered Jude. "I heard him say he was going to be with Abba."

"Ok…" I agreed, hesitantly. Joseph hadn't mentioned that Jesus would go with them, but maybe their friends had children his age that he wanted to visit.

The children and I began the journey home. We played games and talked while we walked among the crowd. We walked until nightfall, and then we set up our tents and sat by the fire. I asked the children what they thought about the Festival, and they re-enacted stories we had talked about. David and Goliath. The Great Flood. Joseph, the dreamer. Moses and the burning bush. Moses and the parting of the Red Sea. Moses and the Ten Commandments.

Finally, through the darkness, we spotted the next traveling group. The children sprung up and ran to meet them, excited for their parents to return. I saw Joseph and Mary and rose to greet them.

"Shalom, my friends," I said. "How was your visit?"

"It was wonderful. It's been some time since we've seen the David family. Their daughter is nearly a teenager now," said Joseph.

"I remember when she was just learning to walk. Now she is a beautiful young lady" Mary smiled.

"Oh, I see," I nodded knowingly. "Perhaps that explains why Jesus stayed with you."

Mary's head jerked up. "What are you talking about?" Immediately, my stomach dropped.

"Didn't Jesus stay with you?"

"No," Joseph said, fear creeping into his voice. "We haven't seen him since this morning." Mary gripped Joseph's arm and began praying aloud.

"The children told me he was with you. I had no idea. I will help you look tonight," I said.

"No," Joseph said firmly. "Tonight, we need rest. Mary and I will have to travel back to Jerusalem tomorrow to search for him. Good night, Hatach." He led Mary away to their tent, speaking low and comfortingly to her.

I watched them walk away and began to pray too for my young friend Jesus.

It was not many more days before I would see him again. Mary and Joseph returned once again to Jerusalem and searched until they found him. I stayed at the location of our first campsite with the other children and waited for them all to return. On the fourth day, we finally saw them from a distance. I squinted against the sun until I saw Jesus' small body between Mary and Joseph. They were holding both of his hands, as if to prevent him from running off again. The children exclaimed over seeing him again and told him about their adventures of the last three days— eating locusts and starting campfires and listening to the wild cats at night. I stood back and watched, breathing a silent prayer of relief that he had been found safely. Finally, one of them asked Jesus where he had been all that time.

"I went to see my Abba, just like I told Jude,"[7] Jesus said. I looked questioningly at Joseph and Mary, but they seemed unfocused, still holding onto Jesus. But I was reminded of that conversation Joseph had with me some time ago where he claimed Jesus was the Son of God, the Promised Messiah. At the time, Joseph's words made no sense to me, but as I watched this young boy grow, I was becoming convinced that he might truly be the Savior.

---

7 Luke2:49, ESV

CHAPTER SIX:

The Friend

Over the next couple of decades, Jesus grew taller and wiser and more blessed by God and man.[8] He continued to call me Papa Hatach, and I had, in a way, stepped in as a father figure after Joseph died. I looked at Jesus like he was my son. Yet Jesus spoke with such wisdom, prayed with such fervor, loved with such compassion; it almost felt like he was the father, and I was the son. As I grew closer to him, I grew closer to God. I began to search my heart to uncover my true motives. Was I becoming obedient to the law of God out of necessity or out of true love for the Word? Jesus had pure intentions. He was a servant, always eager to humble himself and help others. He was quick to listen and slow to speak and even slower to become angry.[9] He cared more about friendships than material wealth. He loved to spend time in nature, soaking in the beauty of Elohim's creation. Jesus and I would often go on walks together as he became a man. One day,

---
8 Luke 2:52, ESV
9 James 1:19, ESV

I shared with him the deaths of Joshua and Mira. He cried with me as I relayed the details of the story. Then, he prayed for me.

We came to a stop, and he said, "Papa Hatach, you have become like a father to me. Especially since my father has passed. The love and support you've shown me and my family over the years has meant so much to me. I love you." He paused here, but I could tell he had more to say.

"Keep your eyes open. I'm preparing to bring a message to Israel that it has been waiting for since the beginning. I will face rejection and turmoil, but I speak to my Father every day and pray for the wisdom and courage to face it." Here, I wrestled again with the story Joseph had told me many years ago about Jesus being God's Son, but I felt almost no resistance to it now. After watching Jesus grow from a young child to a man, it was undeniable that there was something different about him. There was some ordained purpose he carried.

"I pray for you, too. That you will have the faith to believe in my message. You know me, so you know God. Follow me, for no one can come to the Father except through me,"[10] he said.

Almost immediately, I responded, "I will follow you, Jesus." I didn't fully understand what He meant by that

---
10 John 14:6, ESV

message, but I knew agreeing to follow Him was the right response. And I truly meant it. I trusted Jesus and knew I would believe whatever message He would be bringing. He smiled and started walking again. After a few moments of silence, He pointed to a fruit tree about a hundred paces ahead of us up a small hill.

He grinned, and I saw a boy again and not a man. He said, "I'll race you!" Before I could agree, He took off running up the hill, and I found myself chasing after Him, myself feeling like a much younger man again. No knee or hip pain, no aching in my lungs, no uncertainty in my balance. I gained speed as I went until I felt like I was flying up the hill. I laughed loudly at the feeling of pure contentment I had. Suddenly, I saw someone ahead of us by the tree. It was a young man, perhaps in his late twenties like Jesus. He had wavy hair that fell in front of his eyes and a shadow of a beard on his chin. He stood tall and athletic. He reached up and pushed his hair out of his eyes, and I almost stopped in my tracks. He had Mira's eyes, and they were staring right at me. It was Joshua. I picked up speed, determined to reach him before he could vanish. As I got closer, I heard him call out to me, "Run faster! Run with the King!"

I was almost there. I pushed myself even harder and threw myself into his arms. But when I got there, I realized it wasn't Joshua after all. It was Jesus standing there, embracing me. I began to weep as emotions rolled over me. I was confused yet joyous, heartbroken yet exhilarated. As Jesus held me, I felt like I was in the arms of God. I suddenly knew that everything Joseph had told me years ago was true. This man was the Son of God and the Savior of our people. I knew the Messiah had come. I bowed before my friend, the boy I had watched grow into a man, and prayed aloud a prayer of thanksgiving to Adoni for putting this family in my life. I felt Jesus crouch next to me.

"No matter what my future holds, Papa Hatach, our relationship will not end. If you follow me, you will live with me in Paradise one day."[11] This was the same man I had watched grow from a helpless baby, born in a humble stable, yet he was the King of all. Hallelujah, Jesus is Lord!

A few days later, Jesus left to spread his new message. He became quite a wanderer. He would regularly send letters home to Mary and to me too about His journey. He told us of His baptism by His cousin, John, and how the Spirit of God descended in the form of a dove.[12] But soon the letters came to a stop. After not hearing from him for over a month, he finally wrote to us and explained He had removed Himself from all people and even basic comforts like food and housing for forty days. He said it was during

---

11 Luke 23:43, ESV
12 Matthew 3:13-17, ESV

these forty days that He felt most tempted by Satan, but that it was through the strength of the Father that He had held firm to His belief in the Scriptures.[13] As he wrote to us, "Man cannot live on bread alone, but on every Word that comes from the Lord."[14] He wrote to us of His new friends who were traveling with him. He called them His disciples. He told us of the many mornings spent fishing and afternoons spent preaching on mountainsides. With every letter, He reminded us of His love for us and assured us that He was following God's will. He always included a prayer for us. Although He was traveling many miles away, He felt closer to our hearts than ever.

---

13 Matthew 4:1-11, ESV
14 Matthew 4:4, ESV

CHAPTER SEVEN:

The Miracle Man

"Are we there yet?" a small voice piped up next to me. It was James' daughter, Jesus' niece. I smiled, remembering James asking me the same question on our journey to Jerusalem many years ago for the Passover feast.

"We're almost there," I answered. "I think I can see Cana up ahead." She paused, standing on her tiptoes to catch a glimpse of the village in the distance.

"I see it! I see it!" she chirped. "I can't wait to see the bride! And to taste all the yummy food. This is the first time I've been allowed to come along to ta wedding feast, you know. Ima said I was too young when Zahava and Levi got married last year. But now I am grown up. Well, not as much as you, Saba Hatach, but still pretty old."

I laughed. Although I still felt like a young man in many ways, I probably seemed extremely old to this young girl. I had been "Papa" Hatach to her father before her and now "Saba" to her and her baby brother. Life was good. At one time, it would have seemed impossible for that to be true, but now I feel it every day. And what better way to celebrate the fullness of life than to attend a wedding feast?

The next four days passed in a flurry of dancing, singing, feasting, drinking, and celebrating the new lives these two people were beginning together. Mary had been anxious to see Jesus, concerned that His nomadic lifestyle might have caused Him to lose too much weight and become lonely. But He arrived at the feast with His twelve friends, or disciples, and ate and danced and shared stories of His travels. I noticed no trace of loneliness or depression in His demeanor. He smiled, joked, and laughed as loudly as anyone else at the party.

On the fifth day of the feast, rumors started to go around that the host family had run out of wine. More guests had come than they had anticipated. Although this was a great honor, it was a great shame to be unprepared for an abundance of visitors. Mary ran up to Jesus, three servants following behind her, as He was telling me a story of fishing with His disciples out on Lake Gennesaret.

"Jesus, they are out of wine!" she said, almost out of breath with her worry. Jesus and I waited in silence for a further explanation.

"What does this have to do with me?" He asked. "My hour has not yet come."

But Mary seemed not to hear Him. She turned to the servants and said, "Do whatever He tells you."[15]

Jesus cast His eyes up to the heavens and murmured a prayer to El Shaddai. Then, He instructed the servants, "Bring the water jars for the rites of purification."[16] When they had fetched them, Jesus led the servants back to the kitchen with the jars. Mary and I trailed behind.

"Fill the jars with water," said Jesus to the servants. We waited as the large jars were filled. It took some time as each of the six jars held up to thirty gallons of water. When they were filled to the brim, Jesus simply said, "Now draw some out and take it to the master of the feast."[17]

"Oh, but Jesus, he will be expecting wine," Mary said anxiously.

"Do not worry, Ima," He answered and repeated His instruction to the servants. They did as He said and disappeared out of the kitchen with the goblet full of water. Minutes passed with Mary biting her lip to keep herself from speaking out again. I found myself praying to Yahweh that He would not forget His son in this moment.

---

15 John 2:3, ESV
16 John 2:6, ESV
17 John 2:7-8, ESV

Minutes passed before the servants came hurrying back.

"What happened?" Mary burst out, clearly unable to contain herself any longer.

"It was incredible," the chief servant said. "The master of the feast took the goblet from my hand, and I saw it turn in color to the deepest burgundy, and suddenly smelled a floral aroma. He took a sip from the goblet and immediately called for the bridegroom to speak to him. Here, I began to fear that we were going to be caught. But when the bridegroom approached, the master of the feast said, 'Everyone serves the best wine first and when all the guests have drunk too much, they bring out the poor wine. But you surprise me! You have kept the finest wine for now.'[18] And he thanked the bridegroom and spoke a blessing upon their union and has ordered for the rest of this wine to be brought out."

Mary and I stood in amazement and then looked down at the jars around us. They had all turned to wine and we breathed in the aroma of the nicest wine we had ever smelled. We looked to Jesus to ask Him about this thing that He had done, but He had slipped out of the kitchen and rejoined the party.

"It's a miracle," I breathed. It turned out to be the first of many miracles Jesus would work. His glory was

---

18 John 2:9-10, ESV

manifested in this work and in all the others to follow. As we returned home, and Jesus returned to his travels, we received word of many more miracles. Not only from Jesus' letters to us but also from word of mouth from others as He gained a greater following. Crowds of people from Galilee, the Decapolis, Jerusalem, Judea, and all across the Jordan region would follow Him from place to place, listening to His sermons and watching Him perform good works. Some of the stories were so fantastic, they were almost difficult to believe. He healed the sick without even laying hand on them, He made the lame to walk, drove out evil spirits, brought sight to the blind, raised the dead back to life, caused storms to disappear, returned speech to the dumb, fed thousands of people with five small loaves of bread and two fish. As the stories spread, so did Jesus' enemies. Jesus' family and I grew worried that Jesus was attracting a bit too much attention. But He assured us that He was doing all according to His Father's will. We wondered about His future and whether He would be the one to free us from the Romans.

CHAPTER EIGHT:

The Good Shepherd

I continued my carpentry business with the Roman government, making their crosses and making furniture for Nazarenes in my spare time. But I had also begun to travel with Jesus when I was able; sometimes closing my shop for weeks to do so. On one of my journeys with Jesus and the disciples, we came upon a mountainside. Jesus climbed some distance up it, the disciples following him. The rest of us sat down to listen to His sermon. After a quiet prayer, He began.

"Blessed are the poor in spirit, for theirs is the Kingdom of Heaven. Blessed are those who mourn, for they shall be comforted. Blessed are the meek, for they shall inherit the earth. Blessed are those who hunger and thirst for righteousness, for they shall be satisfied. Blessed are the merciful, for they shall receive mercy. Blessed are the pure in heart, for they shall see God. Blessed are the peacemakers, for they shall be called sons of God. Blessed are those who are persecuted for righteousness' sake, for theirs is the Kingdom of Heaven. Blessed are you when others revile you and persecute you and utter all kinds of evil against you falsely on my account. Rejoice and be glad, for your reward is great in Heaven, for so they persecuted the prophets who were before you."[19]

He continued on for hours with this sermon from Yahweh. But these words echoed in my mind even as He went on to talk of other things. "Blessed are those who mourn"? I thought back on my life, the long fifty-eight years behind me. I had certainly done my share of mourning. First, my own father when I was a boy. Then, my mother, months after the birth of my son. Over the years, I had often wished I still had my parents with me when I needed guidance or advice. Especially when I lost my Joshua and Mira as a young man. That pain, that mourning, still lingered. But I had learned over time to look back on my memories as a gift rather than focusing on how brief our time together felt. I had lost my friend, Joseph, though it seemed too soon to be his time. I had mourned alongside Jesus himself and Mary and their other children. I saw the legacy Joseph was leaving behind and knew it was a good one. I let the memories of my lost loved ones roll over me when something else Jesus began to say caught my attention.

"You have heard that it was said, 'You shall love your

---

[19] Matthew 5:3-12, ESV

neighbor and hate your enemy.' But I say to you, love your enemies and pray for those who persecute you, so that you may be sons of your Father who is in Heaven. For he makes his sun rise on the evil and on the good and sends rain on the just and the unjust. For if you love those who love you, what reward do you have? Do not even the tax collectors do the same? And if you greet only your brothers, what more are you doing than others? Do not even the Gentiles do the same? You therefore must be perfect, as your heavenly Father is perfect."[20]

This too Jesus had already taught me. He taught me to overcome my bitterness at the Roman soldiers who had killed my wife and son. He taught me how to forgive and how to show mercy even to those who had wronged me. I remembered the words of Titus, the prisoner I had visited many years ago when Jesus was still a boy. I remembered how he told me he would pray for Herod despite the fact that he was imprisoned by him. At the time, it seemed incomprehensible. But Jesus had shown me, as he had shown Titus, how this kind of love was possible. I looked around at the crowd around me again. Some of them were stirring uneasily, doubts etched across their faces. These teachings came from a humble Nazarene, not a scribe or Pharisee. I knew what Jesus said now was true. I had mourned, but I had also been blessed. Jesus and the Spirit of God had comforted me. I knew it was possible to love

---
[20] Matthew 5:43-48, ESV

even those who seem unlovable. I wanted to stand up next to Jesus and shout to the crowd that it was all true and that they too could find peace if they followed Him. I prayed quietly to Yahweh that Jesus' words would fall on receptive ears. Jesus talked for hours more, and I prayed all the while.

The next couple of years passed in much the same way. More miracles, sermons, and parables. Jesus would occasionally leave the crowds of people for solitude, fasting, and time with the Father, but He spent most of His time ministering to the least of those. We always expected that He would fall in with the religious leaders or even government officials, but He preferred to stay with common people. Thieves. Tax collectors. Gentiles. Children. He did not discriminate. They flocked to Him. I was reminded of the image of my own father when I was a child. My father, who taught me to look after sheep and care for a flock. He taught me to guide them gently using a rod and staff. He taught me to nurse them when they were lambs and care for them when they were injured. I watched him weep over the smallest ones who died in the winter. I watched him fight off a mountain lion to protect them. Jesus, Friend, and Protector did all this and more for all those in His fold. Once, Jesus wrote to us, saying, "I am the Good Shepherd. I know my own and my own know me, just as the Father knows me and I know the Father; and I lay down my life for the sheep. And I have other sheep that are not of this fold. I must bring them also, and they will listen to my voice. So there will be one flock, one shepherd."[21]

He put into words exactly what I had been imagining. Jesus, the Good Shepherd, was bringing God's people together under His love and protection.

Another letter came not long after. Jesus wrote:

"Do you remember that it is written, 'Fear not, daughter of Zion; behold, your king is coming, sitting on a donkey's colt?'[22] I have fulfilled this prophecy. I rode through the streets of Jerusalem and heard all around me the cries of God's chosen people shouting, 'Hosanna!' and 'Blessed is he who comes in the name of the Lord!' They took off their cloaks and broke away palm branches and laid them on the road before me.[23] I rode through the city until I reached the temple. The chief priests are outraged with me. They think it is blasphemy, what the people are saying. I pray you understand that it is the truth. That I am the Way, the Truth, and the Life. And no one may come to the Father except through me.[24]

"I hope to see you all in Jerusalem for the Passover celebration next week. I miss you all dearly."

---

21 John 10:14-16, ESV
22 Zechariah 9:9 and Matthew 21:5, ESV
23 Matthew 21:8-9, ESV
24 John 14:6, ESV

Of course, Jesus' family and I were already packed for our journey to Jerusalem. We talked excitedly about seeing Jesus again and celebrating together.

CHAPTER NINE:

The Betrayal

Things quickly took a turn for the wors. On the first night of the Feast of Unleavened Bread, Jesus was taken captive. His disciple, James, son of Zebedee, told us what happened. Jesus and His twelve disciples had eaten the traditional Passover meal together in a man's home in the city. Jesus had told the men one of them would be His betrayer. The disciples were shocked and confused, each one asking, "Is it I, Rabbi?"

He had answered "you have said so" when Judas asked.[25] The men remained confused. What did it mean that Judas would betray Him? But Jesus had quickly moved on. As they were eating, Jesus took the unleavened bread from the table and blessed it. He passed it around for the disciples to eat, saying "this is my body." Then, he took a cup of wine and passed it around for all to drink, saying "this is my blood."[26] He instructed them to follow this tradition in place of the Passover meal.

---

25 Mark 26:25, ESV
26 Mark 14:22-24, ESV

Following their dinner, Jesus led them to Gethsemane. James and his brother and Peter joined Jesus, and He asked them to remain with Him and watch as He went off to pray. But after the long day, the disciples were tired, so they fell asleep. Jesus returned and said, "Can you not keep watch with me one hour? Watch and pray that you may not enter into temptation."[27] He went off again to pray in the garden, but again when He returned, He had to wake them up. Once more, He went away to pray and once more they fell asleep. This time, he said, "See, the hour is at hand, and the Son of Man is betrayed into the hands of sinners."[28]

Almost as soon as He had said this, Judas approached with a crowd of priests and elders. Judas approached Jesus like a friend, kissing Him on the cheek. Jesus smiled back at Him, but His eyes were full of sorrow. "My friend," he said. "Do what you came to do." And the priests and servants who were with him approached to seize Jesus. All of a sudden, Peter drew his sword and cut off the ear of the servant who had grabbed Jesus by the arm. The servant fell to the ground, clutching the side of his head, and a pool of blood began to spread across their feet.[29]

"Run, Jesus!" Peter cried, still brandishing his sword. But Jesus did not run. Instead, He rebuked Peter and told

---

27 Mark 14:37-38, ESV
28 Mark 14:39-42, ESV
29 Matthew 26:48-51, ESV

him to put away his sword. He got down on His knees and touched the face of the wounded man. Instantly, his screams stopped. All who were there watched in amazement as his ear grew back in its place. He allowed himself to be led away.[30]

Peter was sent to follow at a distance, so he could see where Jesus was taken. John, the other son of Zebedee, had run to tell the other disciples what had happened, and James had run to tell us.

Having heard James's story, Mary wrung her hands and cried out, "We must pray!"

I remembered a prayer I heard Jesus pray at the Sermon on the Mount. I knelt down. James and Mary fell to their knees beside me. I began to pray, "Our Father in Heaven, hallowed be your name. Your Kingdom come; your will be done on Earth as it is in Heaven. Give us this day our daily bread, and forgive us our debts as we also have forgiven our debtors. And lead us not into temptation, but deliver us from evil. Amen."[31]

Then, there was nothing to do but wait for an update from Peter. We sat quietly all night, each of us praying silently and trying to keep calm. I tried to mean what I had prayed. To mean that I wanted God's will even if it was not what I really wanted. It was hard, though. When

---

30 Matthew 26:52-56, ESV
31 Matthew 6:9-13, ESV

I imagined Jesus mocked by religious leaders or sitting in a prison cell or beaten by soldiers, I wanted to break down. This man that I had once seen like a son, came to rely on as a friend, and trusted as my Savior could not be imprisoned. Or worse. I couldn't even think of it.

Suddenly, we heard a knocking at the door. I flew to open it, and Peter rushed in. He looked weary and troubled. My heart fell, as if I knew he bore no good news.

Mary seemed strangely calm as she asked, "What have they done with him?"

Peter said, "I followed the men as they led Jesus through the city. They brought him to the high priest, Caiaphas. I blended in with the guards in the courtyard to listen to all that was happening. The council of men who brought Jesus in called for witnesses. They were looking for false testimony so that He could be put to death. Man after man called out false witnesses against Him, but nothing was severe enough to satisfy the council. Eventually, two men came forward saying, 'I heard this man say that he could destroy the temple of God and rebuild it in three days.' The High Priest Caiaphas pounced on Him like a lion pounces on his prey. He demanded that Jesus deny it or provide an explanation, but Jesus stood silently. The crowd jeered at him,"[32] Peter began to cry as he remembered it all.

---

32 Matthew 26:57-61, ESV

"Jesus' silence seemed to make the high priest more angry. He asked him, 'Are you truly the Christ, the Son of God?' I prayed Jesus would continue with His silence, but He raised His head to look Caiaphas in the eyes and said, 'You have said so.' Then, Caiaphas made a great show of his distress at hearing this. He tore his robes and his hair and cried, 'It is blasphemy! It is blasphemy!' Some began to strike Jesus, mocking him and demanding that he give them a prophecy and spitting in His face. Caiaphas asked for the council's judgment, and they answered without hesitation: "he deserves death."[33]

Mary's calm broke. She covered her face with her hands and began to moan, a low, guttural sound that wrenched my gut when I heard it. I heard a voice say, "Where is he now?" I was startled when I realized I had asked the question.

Peter sank onto a nearby cushion, looking too weak to stand. "They're taking Him to the governor, Pontius Pilate, for an official government sentence."

"We must go to Him," I said.

"Yes, we must," said James, son of Zebedee. "And we will have to hurry."

Mary and Peter nodded their agreement. Together, the four of us walked to the governor's headquarters to watch

---

[33] Matthew 26:62-66, ESV

the trial take place.

As we walked, Mary kept repeating, "He is innocent. Surely, they will see He is innocent." None of us could bring ourselves to answer her.

When we arrived at the governor's headquarters, the trial was already underway. We walked into the place and gasped at the sight. Pilate stood at the front of the crowd, with Jesus shackled at his feet. The entire space was filled with Jewish people. They had come to the city to celebrate the Passover and were instead watching God's Son be sentenced. A line of people had formed in the center of the throng, witnesses speaking out against Jesus. It was clear this had been going on for some time before we got here, yet there were still dozens in line to speak.

"He claims to be God's Son!"

"He teaches things that go against the Word of God!"

"He threatened to destroy the Temple!"

"He violated the Sabbath!"

"He says He is the King of the Jews! He is planning a rebellion against the Roman government!"

"He practices sorcery!"

The accusations arose one at a time, each one like a stone hurled onto Jesus' back. Yet He remained silent, as

Peter said he had done before Caiaphas.[34]

Pilate stretched out his hands, motioning for the crowd to fall silent. He looked down at Jesus, who was lying before him with his eyes closed. Praying. "Are you the King of the Jews?" he asked.

Jesus opened His eyes. "You have said so."[35]

The crowd roared again, "Traitor to Rome! Treachery!"

Pilate lifted his hands again, urging silence. "You say this man is guilty, but I can find no guilt in Him. Do not protest, listen! I find no guilt in Him, but I will send Him to Herod as He is a Galilean and under His jurisdiction."[36]

"Herod!" I exclaimed, turning to the disciples in surprise. "They would send Him to Herod for His crimes?"

"It is surprising," said John thoughtfully. "But clearly Pilate is too much of a coward to make a ruling that would upset the people but too weak to declare him innocent."

Jesus was led out of the court by soldiers. Behind Him trailed the chief priests and scribes, the crowd of His opposers, and His followers at the very back. We walked through the city to the palace where Herod was residing. A messenger had run ahead to inform him of the approaching matter. When we all arrived, Herod was

---

34 Matthew 27:12, ESV
35 Matthew 27:11, ESV
36 Luke 22:6-7, ESV

waiting by the gate with two servants, dressed in splendid robes and resting his hands on his enormous stomach. His face was darkened with an expression of contempt. I knew this man would not find favor with Jesus. He did not find favor with anyone who threatened his authority.

The trial by Herod went no better than any of the others. Herod questioned Jesus for hours with the religious officials throwing in their accusations at the same time. All the same questions and accusations as before. The soldiers standing by mocked Jesus: "If you're really God's Son, why don't you break free from those shackles?" Jesus stood silent like all the other times. Occasionally, He would close His eyes and move His lips like He was praying. But Jesus gave no answer to Herod or the soldiers.

Herod finally threw his hands up in defeat. He cried, "This man claims to be king of the Jews, yet He looks nothing like a king. We will dress Him in the finest clothes and see if He looks more like a king then." He ordered a servant standing nearby to fetch silk dressing gowns from his own wardrobe. I looked down, embarrassed, as the soldiers forced Jesus' arms through the sleeves and tied it tightly around His thin waist.[37]

"Hail, the king of the Jews!" cried Herod. The crowd picked up the chant and those near to Jesus hurled things

---

37 Luke 22:8-12, ESV

THE BETRAYAL

at Him, their shoes or fruit from their lunches. Mary cried silently beside me, and I reached out an arm to support her. While the crowd jeered at Jesus, I sang quietly so that only Mary and I could hear:

> *"God is our refuge and strength,*
> *A very present help in trouble.*
> *Therefore, we will not fear,*
> *Though the earth gives way,*
> *Though the mountains be moved into the heart of the sea,*
> *Though its waters roar and foam*
> *Though the mountains tremble at its swelling.*
> *The Lord of hosts is with us;*
> *the God of Jacob is our fortress.*
> *He says, 'Be still and know that I am God;*
> *I will be exalted among the nations,*
> *I will be exalted in the earth.'"*[38]

Mary joined in at the end and together we sang this psalm and prayed that the Lord would show His power and end this suffering. Finally, seeming bored with Jesus' lack of response to his mockery, Herod declared that he would send Jesus back to Pilate and leave the decision of His punishment to Him. Once again, we followed the procession through the streets. Jesus was half-dragged,

---
[38] Psalms 46:1-3, 10-11, ESV

half-carried back to Pilate's headquarters with an even larger trail of observers following Him this time.

Pilate seemed hardly able to look at Jesus. He spoke to the crowd, saying "Look at this man! He has done nothing deserving of death!" My heart soared for one moment, thinking Jesus would be released, and we could return home and forget any of this ever happened. "I will punish Him for His crimes, but He will be released," Pilate finished.[39]

The crowd booed him. Someone yelled out, "Release Barabbas to us instead!"[40]

"Who's Barabbas?" I wondered aloud.

The man standing in front of me turned around. "You haven't heard of him? He led the riot last year against the Romans. And he—"

Pilate began to speak again. "Release Barabbas? A known murderer? A man who led an insurrection in the city?[41] He destroyed homes and businesses alike in his riot, and you want him to be released instead of this innocent man? Let me release Jesus and keep Barabbas in prison, where he belongs."

A religious leader stepped forward from the crowd.

---

39 Luke 23:13-16, ESV
40 Luke 23:18, ESV
41 Luke 23:19, ESV

"Don't forget, Pilate. It is the custom to release one prisoner during the time of Passover.[42] We choose Barabbas to be released. Crucify this Jesus!"

"Crucify him! Crucify him!"[43] The crowd echoed back. They began to push towards the stage where Pilate was standing.

Pilate sighed, looking defeated. My heart sank again. I watched as he turned and spoke quietly to a servant on his left and then to a soldier on his right. Both men disappeared, and the crowd fell silent.

The soldier returned quickly with Barabbas by his side. I gasped at the sight of the murderer. He looked dirty and unkempt after years in prison. His face was blackened with dirt, but you could see his eyes gleaming through his dirt-caked face and bushy eyebrows. They did not look repentant. The contrast between his evil look and Jesus' calm, peaceful expression was stark. It was obvious which of these men was the true criminal. The soldier released the man from his shackles and shoved him towards the crowd. They cheered as they received him.

Then, the servant returned, carrying a basin of water. Pilate dipped his hands into the water. Scrubbing his hands together, he said, "I am innocent of this man's

---

42 Matthew 27:15, ESV
43 Matthew 27:23, ESV

blood. It is your responsibility."[44] As the crowd cheered their approval, Pilate handed Jesus over to be flogged by the soldiers and disappeared inside, apparently unable to watch the proceedings anymore.

---

[44] Matthew 27:24-25, ESV

CHAPTER TEN:

The Crucifixion

Tears streamed down my face as I watched the soldiers beat Jesus. As they whipped Him, He cried out in agony, and I heard in my mind the sound of my Mira screaming as the soldiers wrestled our son from her arms. It was almost too much to bear. They were killing my son again. But I couldn't leave. I had to be there for Jesus, as He had been there for me for so many years. He had been my comfort. Maybe I could be His now.

They had stripped off His gowns from Herod and thrown a scarlet robe on Him. Someone from the crowd had twisted together a crown of thorns and passed it to the soldiers. They jammed it on His head, and I saw the blood seep from the deep scratches it made on His scalp. Someone placed a staff in His hand, and all those gathered around bowed down to the ground in mockery.

"Hail, king of the Jews!" They cried, spitting on Him. A soldier snatched the staff out of His hand and struck

Him on the head. Jesus fell to the ground. The soldier struck Him again. And again. And again. As His blood flowed, the sharp smell of iron filled the air.

"Why don't You call Your angels to save You?" They asked. Jesus did not answer.[45]

Jesus' letter from the previous week came to mind. Were these not the same people who cried "Hosanna!" and laid down their own robes for Jesus to walk on? Were these not the same people who had followed Him around for years, hoping to touch the edge of His robe?

Having beaten Him until He was almost unrecognizable, the soldiers decided it was time for the crucifixion. They brought out the cross. When I saw it, I felt sick to my stomach. I saw the streaks running through it, the imperfections. Just like Jesus had shown me when He was a young carpenter in my shop. I recognized my own work. I had made the cross Jesus would die on. I ran to the back of the crowd and fell to my knees. I vomited as regret and guilt wracked my body.

"Papa Hatach." The voice brought me back. It was not Jesus but His brother, Joses. He had followed me through the crowd and extended his hand to help me up.

"You don't understand," I said in a whisper. "I made that cross. I helped kill him."

---

45 Matthew 27:27-30, ESV

THE CRUCIFIXION

"You didn't know," said Joses. "It was just a job. You didn't know."

I vowed at that moment to close my carpentry shop. I would sell all my wood and all my tools and return to shepherding like my father. Like Jesus, the Good Shepherd.

"Come along," said Joses. "They are taking him to Golgotha."[46]

I let him help me to my feet. "Where's your mother?" I asked, suddenly worried. I had forgotten Mary in my panic.

"She's with James and the disciples. We'll find them," he said. He kept his hand on my arm as we walked behind the crowd to Golgotha. I don't know if his hand was there to keep me steady or to keep him grounded. I think we both needed it.

We reached the top of the hill and watched as the Roman soldiers drove the cross into the ground and then raised Jesus up onto it. As they drove the nails into His hands, He cried out and said, "Abba, forgive them, for they do not know what they are doing!"[47]

I marveled that even now forgiveness was on His mind. But as He hung there, his arms outspread, it was

---
46 Matthew 27:33, ESV
47 Luke 23:24, ESV

almost the perfect picture of the way he had lived His whole life: arms open wide. Full of mercy. Full of love. Full of forgiveness. Above His head, the soldiers nailed a plaque reading, "This is Jesus, the king of the Jews."[48] It hurt me to read it because I knew it was just a continuation of their mockery. But at the same time, I knew it was true. I knew He was the Son of God and the true King.

I held out for a miracle. The criminal on Jesus' side mocked him, saying, "Aren't you the promised Messiah? Save yourself! Save us!"[49] I prayed that it might be possible. That God might intervene and show His power and save Jesus in the end. As darkness fell over the land, I knew it would not be true. Although it was noon, and the sun should have been high above us, there was complete darkness.[50] The world mourned with us at the death of Jesus. It continued for three agonizing hours until he called out, "Abba, into your hands I commit my spirit." With that, he breathed his last.[51]

I had been in the same inn where Jesus was born. I had watched Him grow up and felt like He was the second son I craved. I saw Him turn into a minister and a healer. He changed my life and the lives of countless others. I prayed again, "Yahweh, I do not understand why you are taking Jesus so soon. He had so much more good work He could

---

[48] Matthew 27:37, ESV
[49] Luke 23:39, ESV
[50] Luke 23:44, ESV
[51] Luke 23:46, ESV

have done. But I have seen your hand at every point in my life, and I trust you."

I stood by and watched as they took Him down from the cross and wished it were I rather than Joseph of Arimathea who had volunteered a tomb. A resting place for Jesus. I walked with Mary to the tomb and watched as they wrapped His body in linen and laid Him there. We cried together until we had no tears left to cry. Then, we continued on in silence. The sun had returned to its rightful place, but I almost wished it hadn't. It didn't seem fitting that it should still shine with Jesus dead.

Mary and I were staying with the Zebedee family in Jerusalem. We returned to their home and prepared for the Sabbath the next morning. We would still worship God and sing praises to Him despite our loss. I had learned already that turning away from El Kannah in times of suffering only caused more heartbreak. This time, I was determined to keep my faith.

CHAPTER ELEVEN:

One More Race

Mary, the mother of the disciple James, burst into the Zebedee house. Her face was flushed and excited, seeming very out of place among this house of mourners. She had gone with Joanna and Mary Magdalene to take their prepared spices to Jesus' tomb for His body.

"Hatach," she panted. "Hatach, he wasn't there. I already went to the disciples and told them. He wasn't there!"

I stood up and crossed the room in a moment. "What do you mean? Who wasn't there?"

"Jesus! He's gone."

Were the soldiers really so cruel? Could they not even honor the proper burial customs for this man? Or was it the Pharisees? Maybe they had removed His body and defiled it even in death. My heart burned with rage until I almost didn't hear what Mary said next.

"He's alive!"

"Mary, that can't be," I put my hand on her arm and spoke gently. "You were there with us. You saw Him die."

She shook my hand off. "No, I mean it. I saw Him. He's alive!"

Jesus' mother had heard Mary's cries and walked in the room. At this, she stopped dead in her tracks. "Alive?" she breathed.

"Mary, I think we're going to need your full story," I said to her. I led her to the table and placed a warm cup of halitot in front of her. She took a deep breath and began speaking.

"I woke early this morning and met up with Joanna and Mary Magdalene. We walked together to the tomb, carrying our herbs and spices, and recalling memories of Jesus.[52] When we got to the tomb, the stone had been rolled to the side. We peered inside, thinking someone else was already there, preparing the body. But it was empty. All that was inside were the linen cloths that had been used to wrap His body. We even looked around outside the tomb, but there was nothing.

---

52 Luke 24:10, ESV

"Mary Magdalene volunteered to run to tell the disciples since she is the youngest of us.[53] So she ran back and told Peter and the others that Jesus' body had been taken from the tomb. Meanwhile, Joanna and I waited at the tomb. When Mary came back, she brought two of the disciples with her. They too saw that the tomb was empty, and the linen clothes folded where the body should be. They wept with us and said they would tell the others. So, the disciples left, and us women were walking back to the city when we met a man on the road.

"'Greetings,' he called. But he was too far off for us to truly see him. As we walked closer, we all gasped in shock. It was Jesus![54] I saw him with my own eyes. I clasped His hands, fell at His feet, and worshiped. I have seen the risen Lord! He said He will visit the disciples tonight and again in Galilee. We must go to Galilee, so we can see Him!" She finished exuberantly.

"Are you certain?" asked Jesus' mother, still hesitant to believe it.

Mary clasped her hands and looked straight into her eyes. "Mary, I am more certain of it than I have been of anything my entire life. I know that Jesus is alive."

The two women jumped up and down and hugged each

---

53 John 20:2, ESV
54 Matthew 28:8-10, ESV

other tightly. I was still numb from the shock, but it was beginning to transform into pure joy. God had worked His miracle after all. Jesus was alive, and we would see Him again soon.

We packed up our things quickly and began the journey to Galilee to see Him. Jesus' mother asked Mary, wife of Zebedee, countless questions as we traveled, wanting to solidify every detail in her mind before she saw her son again.

"How did He look? You said He still had scars in His hands? Did He say where to go once we reach Galilee? Did He seem changed to you? More sad, I mean. Or happier, I suppose. Did He mention being hungry? Did He ask about me or His brothers?"

Mary answered each of her questions patiently, and we all chatted together about what we would like to do with Jesus when we saw Him again.

"I want to listen to his stories," said the disciples' mother. "When He would visit with James and John, they always had the most interesting stories from their travels. Once, Jesus told me that they were in a boat on the Sea of Galilee. Jesus was actually sleeping when suddenly a storm came up. James and John told me it was the biggest storm they had ever been in, but Jesus just kept sleeping.

All the disciples were scared the ship would sink, so they woke Jesus up and said, 'Save us! We are going to drown!' Jesus said He looked around at the wind and waves and rebuked them, and the storm died down at once. I asked Jesus what happened next, and He shrugged and said, 'I went back to sleep.'"[55]

Mary and I laughed at the story. Then Mary said, "I want to see Him with His family again. With His brothers, nieces, and nephews. He was always so good with children. Often, His disciples would try to keep the crying babies and clamoring children away from Him, but He always welcomed them just as He welcomed everyone."

I smiled, remembering when He had blessed the little children at the Sermon on the Mount. The women asked what I wanted to do, and I told them I just wanted to share a meal with Him one more time. But I kept my deepest wish to myself. I wanted to run with Jesus again. I felt so connected with Him when we ran together. I just wanted to race one more time. To feel like a young man again and fly across the ground. To collapse out of breath with Him and hear Him say, "Not too bad, Papa Hatach."

When we had returned home, we parted ways, unsure of what to do while we waited to hear from the disciples. Mary went home to her children. I went home to my

---

[55] Mark 4:35-41, ESV

carpentry shop. I walked through the door and looked around, still disgusted with myself and my crosses. Over the next several days, I sold all my wood and carpentry tools and most of the finished pieces I had stored. I kept a small bowl I had made in the "Jesus style." Full of scarred wood.

I made it a habit to eat out of this bowl as often as I could. One day about a week after I had returned home to Nazareth, I was sitting and enjoying lentil soup out of my scarred bowl. Suddenly, I heard a rustling sound behind me. I whirled around, confused at who could have gotten into my house. And there was Jesus.

He looked radiant. Almost as if He were standing in front of the sun, and it was glowing around Him. He was beaming from ear to ear. His arms outstretched, ready to receive me. I saw the nail-scarred hands that Mary had described. I remembered the soldiers beating Him and knew He must bear scars all across His back, too. But when I looked in His face, I saw the same Jesus I had known as a toddler. I let out a gasping sob and rushed to Him.

He laughed as I threw my arms around me and said, "It's good to see you too, Papa Hatach." We stood like that, embracing one another, for several minutes. Each of us thanking God and blessing the other person. Finally, we separated and stood at arm's length.

He spoke again. "I wanted to thank you, Papa Hatach. I know you went through great grief when your son died. You didn't know it at the time, but your son was killed so that I could live. King Herod was looking for me that night. He had heard rumors of the birth of a boy who would grow to be king, and he was determined to kill all the infant boys to put a stop to it. My parents were warned in a dream to hide me away in Egypt to escape the killing. But so many young boys were killed. I'm sorry you had to suffer like that. But when I was killed on the cross, it was so that all could live. That is why my life was protected as a baby. That is why I was put on this Earth. To die. I became the sacrifice that the world needed. For those who believe in me, their sins will be forgiven. No other sacrifices need to be made. All that is needed is to repent and have faith."

I believed. I had faith. I had seen with my own eyes the wonders Jesus had worked and felt His spirit change my life. I knew He was God's Son; I believed He was the Messiah, and I knew I had been saved. I felt a freedom and a joy I had never known before. I knelt to my knees and said, "It is I who should be thanking You, Jesus. You have saved me in every way possible. You brought me joy and comfort when I needed it, and you have saved my soul."

He smiled at me and asked, "Want to race?"

And we ran. One last time, we ran. I felt the glory of God around us when He laughed as I, an old man now, tried to catch Him. "Keep running, my friend! Run the race and receive your heavenly prize," he called.

And suddenly, He was gone. I smiled up to the heavens and spoke to my Joshua. "I did it, son. I ran with the King."